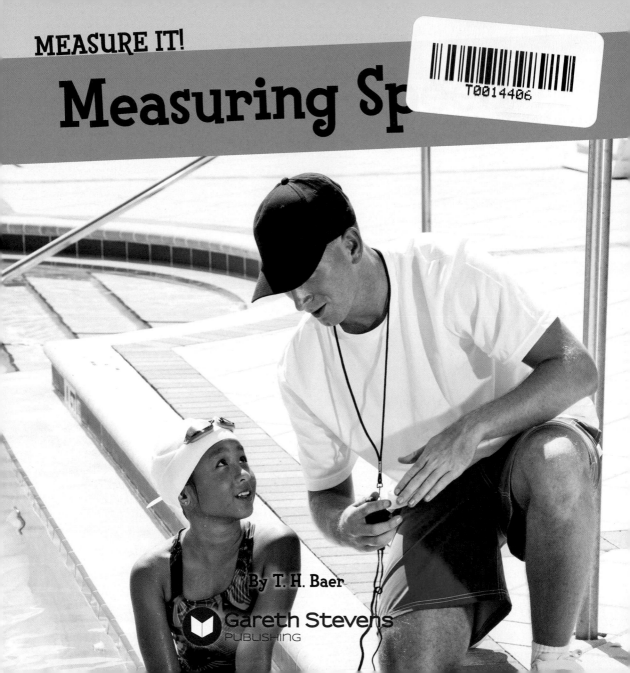

# MEASURE IT!

# Measuring Sp

By T. H. Baer

## Gareth Stevens
PUBLISHING

Please visit our website, www.garethstevens.com. For a free color catalog of all our high-quality books, call toll free 1-800-542-2595 or fax 1-877-542-2596.

Library of Congress Cataloging-in-Publication Data

Baer, T. H., author.
 Measuring speed / T.H. Baer.
     pages cm — (Measure it!)
 Includes index.
 Audience: 6-7.
 Audience: K.
 ISBN 978-1-4824-3864-2 (pbk.)
 ISBN 978-1-4824-3865-9 (6 pack)
 ISBN 978-1-4824-3866-6 (library binding)
 1.  Speed—Measurement—Juvenile literature.  I. Title. II. Series: Measure it! (Gareth Stevens Publishing)
 QC137.52.B34 2016
 531'.112—dc23

                              2015028097


Published in 2016 by
**Gareth Stevens Publishing**
111 East 14th Street, Suite 349
New York, NY 10003

Copyright © 2016 Gareth Stevens Publishing

Designer: Laura Bowen
Editor: Ryan Nagelhout

Photo credits: Cover, p. 1 kali9/E+/Getty Images; pp. 2–24 (background texture) style_TTT/Shutterstock.com; p. 5 iofoto/Shutterstock.com; p. 7 rangizzz/Shutterstock.com; p. 9 Peter Gardner/Dorling Kindersley/Getty Images; p. 11 Richard Thornton/Shutterstock.com; p. 13 James Bowyer/Shutterstock.com; p. 15 Sergey Novikov/Shutterstock.com; p. 17 Stuart Monk/Shutterstock.com; p. 19 Loskutnikov/Shutterstock.com; p. 21 Italianvideophotoagency/Shutterstock.com.

Printed in the United States of America

CPSIA compliance information: Batch #CW16GS: For further information contact Gareth Stevens, New York, New York at 1-800-542-2595.

# Contents

**Boldface** words appear in the glossary.

# How Fast Is Fast?

Do you like to run? You may be faster than your friends, but how fast are you actually running? The measurement of how fast something is moving is called speed. Let's find out how to measure it!

Speed is measured by figuring out how far something travels over a length of time. We measure time in seconds, minutes, and hours. Sixty seconds is a minute. There are 60 minutes in an hour. A clock keeps track of seconds, minutes, and hours.

## Speed Tools

A special clock called a stopwatch can measure time very **accurately**. It even keeps track of small parts of seconds, called fractions. To use a stopwatch, you press a button when what you're timing starts to move. You press the button again to stop it at the end.

## Miles to Go

A mile (mi) is a **unit** in the US customary system. A mile is 5,280 feet (ft). Miles measure the distance an object travels. When you combine distance and time, you get speed. If a train travels 80 miles in an hour, it's moving 80 miles per hour (mph).

$$\frac{80 \text{ miles}}{1 \text{ hour}} = 80 \text{ mph}$$

Hours and miles are used even over short distances. If a car travels 10 miles in 30 minutes, what is its **average** speed? Thirty minutes is half an hour, so in a full hour, the car would travel 20 miles. Its speed is 20 miles per hour!

speedometer

$$\frac{10 \text{ miles} + 10 \text{ miles}}{30 \text{ min} + 30 \text{ min}} = \frac{20 \text{ miles}}{1 \text{ hour}} = 20 \text{ mph}$$

# Measuring Metric

The metric system uses kilometers (km) to measure distance. There are 1,000 meters (m) in a kilometer. Speed is measured in kilometers per hour (km/h). Kilometers can be **converted** into miles. One mile equals about 1.6 kilometers.

Track events are often measured using meters.

One morning, a bus traveled 20 kilometers on its way to school. The bus got to school in 30 minutes. We know 30 minutes is one half of an hour. What was the average speed of the bus?

$$\frac{20\ km + 20\ km}{30\ min + 30\ min} = \frac{40\ km}{1\ hour} = 40\ km/h$$

# On the Water

We use a different unit to track speed when on water. A nautical mile is based on a measurement of Earth's **circumference**. A nautical mile is about 1.15 miles in US customary units and about 1.85 kilometers in metric units.

circumference

The speed of boats and **submarines** is measured by how many nautical miles they travel in an hour. This measurement is called a knot. Unlike the way different countries use either miles or kilometers to measure speed, everyone uses the knot to measure speed on the water!

# Glossary

**accurately:** in a manner free from mistakes

**average:** the figure you get when you add a group of numbers and then divide the total by the number of numbers

**circumference:** the total distance around a circle or ball

**convert:** to change from one unit to another

**submarine:** a ship meant to travel underwater

**unit:** a uniform amount used for measuring

# For More Information

## Books

Paris, Stephanie. *Vroom! Speed and Acceleration.* Huntington Beach, CA: Teacher Created Materials, 2013.

Parker, Steve. *Speed.* New York, NY: Sandy Creek, 2013.

Thompson, Helen. *Travel Math.* Broomall, PA: Mason Crest, 2014.

## Websites

**Kids Math: Units of Measurement**
*ducksters.com/kidsmath/units_of_measurement_glossary.php*
Find out more about different units of measurement here.

**Measuring Boat Speed**
*pbskids.org/zoom/activities/sci/measuringboatspeed.html*
Learn how to measure boat speed on this PBS Kids website.

**Time Facts for Kids**
*sciencekids.co.nz/sciencefacts/time.html*
Find out more facts about how time is measured on this site.

# Index